FOR THE
Love
OF
Greens

*Making Mealtimes a Whole
Lot Healthier, Green, and Fun!*

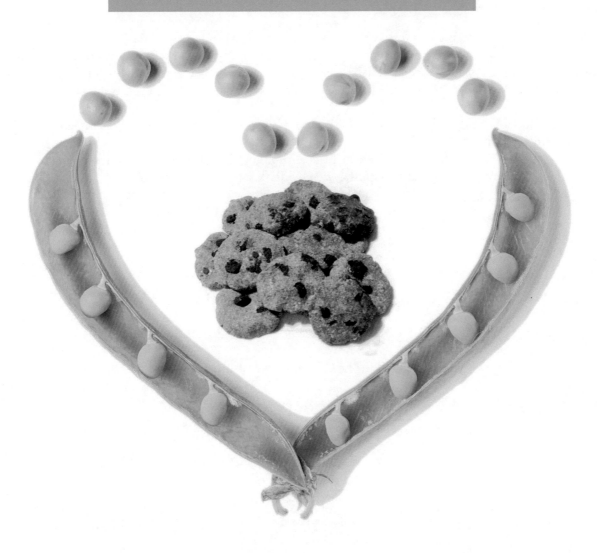

Cristina Cavalieri D'Oro

Balboa Press books may be ordered through booksellers or by contacting:

Balboa Press
A Division of Hay House
1663 Liberty Drive
Bloomington, IN 47403
www.balboapress.com
1 (877) 407-4847

ISBN: 978-1-4525-2087-2 (sc)
ISBN: 978-1-4525-2088-9 (e)

Library of Congress Control Number: 2014915518

Printed in the United States of America.

Balboa Press rev. date: 10/22/2014

BALBOA
PRESS
A DIVISION OF HAY HOUSE

CONTENTS

INTRODUCTION

One of the things I love is making great meals for my family to enjoy! I love to make meals that will leave them feeling nourished and satiated, all while giving them energy, vitamins, minerals and nutrients. In a nutshell, I love preparing meals that will make them thrive! This may sound pretty easy, but when you have two small kids and one in particular who doesn't like many greens, this calls for creativity!

I am really excited and eager to get this message out there. Providing our children and ourselves with good health is our responsibility! There are more and more people buying convenient, fast food and processed foods. The rise of illnesses is increasing in children and adults. Obesity is on the rise. Food DOES matter and it is with passion that I write this. I know how hard it can be to turn your whole diet around, but a baby step here and one there will add up.

"What should I do for their lunches? I'm so sick of making things, and my kids just complain! I have the feeling of not being good enough or feeling guilty, but still continue with the same routine." Does this sound familiar? There is no need for parental guilt here. We're all doing the best that we know how with the information on hand, but the more we learn, the more we see that something needs to be done. Let's make a shift in a lighthearted way to add more greens in a fun tasty way while eliminating fast and processed foods. It doesn't have to be controlling or forced; eating needs to be enjoyable for the child AND the parent as well!

THE SCOOP ON GREENS

Vegetables, especially green leafy veggies, are loaded with vitamins, minerals, fibers and are alkalizing, which means they balance the acidity that is predominant from our processed diets, stressful lives, pollution, etc. Acidity is the root cause of most diseases. Green leafy veggies are wholesome, nourishing and exactly what is lacking in most children's (and adults) diets. Having different varieties of greens every day helps our body to run smoothly. Learning to incorporate these greens in our meals give us a healthy body and an immune system that works for us.

The idea is to add in more variety. A larger quantity of greens, along with foods that will strengthen and nourish the body, will give us a better understanding of how food really does affect us and make us more aware of our body's signals.

> "Your children will see what you're all about by
> what you live rather than what you say."
> Wayne W. Dyer

It is essential for us, as parents, to know this because we can practice what we preach and secondly, we're confident in our ability to provide healthy foods to our children. By doing this, we're building a strong foundation for ourselves, our children and future generations.

I know it might seem overwhelming or challenging at first if this is a new way of eating for your family. There are so many different diets out there from vegan to raw foodist, paleo to macrobiotics and so much more in between. There is so much advice out there about what we should and shouldn't eat. But one thing everyone does agree with is that fresh green vegetables need to be abundant in our diet, which is the opposite of the Standard American Diet. My intention for this book is for you to incorporate more greens in everything, so that it just comes naturally and simply into your lifestyle.

What do I mean by "everything?" Well, just that—EVERYTHING! Cakes? Yup, greens can go there. Ice cream? Oh, yes—definitely! There really is no limit to where and how many greens you can add to your meals. My intention is also for you to choose wholesome, "real" food and eliminate processed foods and sugars. This is not a fad or a diet. This is adding vitality into our life! Our body needs proper fuel and it gets it through what we feed our bodies, our minds and our souls. What we put in, will come out, so let's keep it nourishing and positive! Making this a lifestyle choice for the whole family is really the way to go so that the whole family can be conscious of what they put in their bodies. Health is our birthright!

"The first wealth is health."
Ralph Waldo Emerson

THE BEGINNING

According to Dr. Joel Fuhrman, "When you have a child, you have the unique opportunity to mold a developing person. One of your greatest gifts to them can be a disease-resistant body created from excellent food choices beginning at youth. Ear infections, strep throats, allergies, attention deficit hyperactivity disorders (ADD or ADHD), and even autoimmune diseases can be prevented by sound nutritional practices early in life."[1]

The easiest and most effective way to have children eat lots of wholesome foods is to start them off on these foods in the first place. From the foods the mother eats, while she is pregnant and breastfeeding to the child's first foods, having lots of greens and whole foods is important. What do I mean by whole foods? Foods that haven't been processed or refined. Foods that our great-grandparents would recognize as actual food. These are foods that don't have a long list of ingredients that we're not able to pronounce.

"Don't eat anything your great-great grandmother wouldn't recognize as food… There are a great many food-like items in the supermarket your ancestors wouldn't recognize as food…stay away from these."
Michael Pollan

Avoid introducing any processed foods, fast foods or any items with refined sugars and chemicals, PERIOD. There is nothing healthy about them. Yes, they're cheaper. Yes, they're convenient, but at what cost? Foods that are introduced are foods that the parents eat. So really take a good look at your diet and see why you eat and crave certain foods. Ask yourself if this food will nourish you.

Refined and artificial sugars affect behavior. It has so many side effects in the long run, and it's addictive. It's best to completely avoid, not only for kids, but for adults as well. There are so many natural alternatives to sweetening up food that refined and artificial sugars are just not needed.

If your kids are older and are already used to processed and refined foods, you can still make it work. Start by increasing the amount of greens and whole foods in the diet and slowly phase out those other items that are not so healthy. By adding more and more of the good stuff, they will generally want less of the other. I know how hard it can be to cut something out that a child really enjoys. After doing an intolerance test for one of my daughters because she developed eczema, we found out a lot of her favorite foods were not that great for her at the moment. So instead of focusing on the foods we couldn't have, **we chose to concentrate on everything else that is available.** When we focus on what we can't have, we feel deprived. Let's get this straight, you can have anything you want, but you're CHOOSING not to; there's a difference. When you focus on what's available to you, you can easily come up with a tasty meal. When you focus on what you cannot have, whatever else you eat will only leave you feeling deprived. So really, change your outlook and increase the foods that nourish and support you.

Other options to making this a smooth transition is to make healthier versions of the foods that you already love and are accustomed to. Every recipe can be altered and made in a healthier version. If you have lots of alternatives on hand, it will prevent wanting to reach for those quick junk food fixes. Talk about it with your kids and see what works best for your family. Of course, this will vary depending the age of your child. This is a family choice, and it's important that you as parents are examples and lead the way in a joyous way but also respect your child's need regarding where they're at.

Naturally, your kids have their own personalities, different tastes and most likely addictions to some of the foods that are being eliminated. So there will be some adjustment period and loving patience needed. With older kids, you can sit down and watch documentaries, like *Hungry for Change, Food Inc.* and *Supersize Me* to name a few. So they can see the effect that food has on their bodies and then they can decide what to do. Watch it together as a family. Not "sit here and watch this!" But more along the lines of, "I would love your opinion on this film, can you watch it with me?" It will take the stress out of the whole matter and make them feel like a part of a choice instead of being told what to do.

Also, talk to them about all the great benefits they will get from a healthy diet, examples; great skin, more energy for the sports games, better focus and concentration for their school work etc.

FROM SEED TO PLATE

If you live in an environment where you're able to grow food, it's a great way to get kids interested in the whole process. When spring rolls around, my daughters love to go in the garden with their grandma and work in it. They learn all the different steps from preparing the soil to picking the vegetables when it is ready. They are also much more inclined to eat these veggies that they harvested and picked themselves. Sprouting is also a great way to see transformation happening right in front of your eyes with living foods and is a great science experiment.

Involving kids in the preparation of food and the cooking process gets them excited about what they will eat. It can unleash some creativity by trying new spices or changing up the recipe a bit. Kids love to help if given a chance, including washing foods, chopping foods and especially sampling the food to see if there is anything that needs to be added! Singing or putting on some music always adds more of a festive feel as well.

READING LABELS

What most people don't realize is that one of the major reasons they would buy something at the grocery store is because of marketing. There are so many choices at the grocery store of foods that are specifically marketed for kids, but are these choices the right ones? Usually, they're not, and it is important to read the ingredients list and know exactly what you're getting. The general rule is that if you're not able to pronounce the ingredient and don't know what it is, stay away from it. If it has more than 5 ingredients, you don't need to have it, and if it's been sitting on a shelf for years, skip it! Also, packaging has become really tricky lately. It can be labelled healthy, gluten-free or organic, but that doesn't necessarily mean you should be having it, so read the full ingredient list. Like Michael Pollan says, "If it's a plant, eat it. If it was made in a plant, don't."

TIME

One of the most frequent complaints I hear is: "But I don't have time to cook or prepare foods." Yes, you do. With proper planning, you definitely do. You need to take and *make* the time for this. It's your health, and it is a top priority. Here are some tips to get more organized so cooking time fits into your schedule.

- Create a weekly menu plan: This is great, as it gives you the chance to balance and alternate your meals instead of wondering what you will do and end up always having the same thing or grabbing something quick. You get variety and it's less stressful.
- Cook once, eat twice: Make a big batch of food for lunch and have the leftovers for dinner. You can spice it up by adding a different veggie or salad with your meal.
- Cooking day: This is an option where you can set aside a cooking day and prepare big batches of food and freeze it for those days that you're in an extra rush and know you won't have time to prepare a meal.
- Schedule cooking into your day: Set aside time in your day for cooking. If you need to schedule it into your calendar, then do so!
- If you really don't enjoy cooking, hire a private chef or a mom's helper. This will free up your time and your family will still get the benefits of a home cooked meal.

This is really one of the biggest gifts you can give your family. Fast food, food that has been on the shelf for months, microwaved dinners and food filled with preservatives are surely quick. But the long-term effects of having these consistently in your diet will show up. If not right away, then later on in life.

IS ORGANIC REALLY BETTER?

Yes, it is! The quality of the foods that we pick also has an impact. Organic produce is grown without pesticides, and no fertilizers are used. Yes, it can get more expensive, but there are ways that can cut the costs.

- Shopping at farmers markets is a great way to eat locally and buy what is in season; your produce will definitely be fresh, all while supporting farmers. Get to know the farmers and find out their practices. Many times, they grow their food organically, but they are just not certified because of the costs.
- Buying the produce wholesale and freezing it (I do this with bananas, mangoes and berries)
- Starting an organic buying club (having a group of friends and buying the foods wholesale and distributing the goods at cost price amongst each other) is a good idea.

But if you're not able to have organic, that shouldn't stop you from eating vegetables. The non-organic produce is still better than not having anything at all. You really need to make your own judgment. If you can't buy some foods organic, then try to buy the foods that have been tested to be the highest in pesticide residues.

This is the dirty dozen 2014 list and the clean 15 from 'Environmental Working Group' website[2].

The Dirty Dozen (in order of contamination) so try to get these organic.
Apples, Strawberries, Grapes, Celery, Peaches, Spinach, Sweet bell peppers, Nectarines, Cucumbers, Cherry tomatoes, Snap peas, Potatoes

The Clean 15 (in order of least contamination)
Avocado, Sweet Corn, Pineapples, Cabbage, Sweet peas, Onions, Asparagus, Mangos, Papaya, Kiwi, Eggplant, Grapefruit, Cantaloupe, Cauliflower, Sweet potatoes

MEAT, EGGS & DAIRY

If your family consumes meat, eggs and dairy, then I would definitely have that as a priority to eat organic. It's best to choose organic, grass-fed, free-range meat/eggs. Not only for the better treatment of animals, but also regarding what they are fed and all the antibiotics that are given to them. Avoid any animals from factory farming and get to know your local farmers, what they feed their animals and how they're raised. "Antibiotics are used in livestock to prevent disease, but they are also used as a protectant and to aid growth. About 29.9 million pounds of antibiotics were sold in 2011 for meat and poultry production, compared with the 7.7 million pounds sold for human use, according to the Pew Charitable Trusts."[3]

MAKE MEAL TIMES PLEASURABLE – Vitamin P

It's not only what you eat, but *how* you eat. Building a healthy relationship with food from the start is so important. Children pick up everything we do or say, so let's be attentive to our thoughts and question them. See if what we're thinking is truly coming from us or habits of our parents' (or adults around us) way of thinking when we were growing up, which may not be beneficial for us anymore.

Listen to your child. If he's not hungry, don't force him to eat. He might not be hungry at the specific time you want him to eat or if he ate some of his food and says he's full, why does he need to have "a couple more bites" for you? This is giving him a couple of messages, namely not to stop eating when he's full and to eat "a couple more bites" just to please someone else. When kids are hungry, they will eat (unless there is a medical condition involved).

Sometimes, they just don't like the food, and that's okay, too. It doesn't mean they will *never* like it, it means they just don't like it right now. According to research, children need to be offered a new food 10-15 times before they eat it. Sometimes it's more, sometimes it's less, so experiment preparing the food in question in different recipes. Let's watch our comments as well, when your child doesn't like something, no need to say "my kid hates broccoli, vegetables etc." Your child hears this and then acts on this and it becomes a reality for them, instead you can say nothing or something like "you don't want this today, that's fine, we can try it another time." An example of this is my daughter never ate salad but one day she took some and liked it, she wrapped her food in it and made it into a sandwich! We do have an agreement though; we need to taste the food before making a decision.

How we eat is just as important as what we eat. If eating is becoming a battle, how effective will the absorption of the food be? This works for us parents as well; children learn from us most of all! Eating is an enjoyable process, so let's leave the guilt, bribing, threats and battles at the door!

When eating, take the time to chew and enjoy your food. I know this might seem like common sense but how often are we eating rushed or with distractions like TV, computer, cell phones and even reading? You will savor the food better, you absorb the nutrition from the food better and you assist your digestion process. You also feel more satisfied after a meal. Enjoy every moment and every bite of it and make chewing your food a big part of eating.

Having rituals and giving thanks always calms everyone and creates a peaceful atmosphere before the meal. We give thanks and light a beeswax candle before our meals. Everyone really enjoys this part. With kids, we can also say, "Thank you, carrot, for providing my body with beta-carotene that makes my eyes see well." You're being thankful AND learning about the many benefits of what the food does for us as well.

SOCIAL PRESSURE

"Be who you are and say what you feel, because those who mind don't matter and those who matter don't mind."
Dr. Seuss

When we are invited at a friend's home or events where I know there will be the regular party foods and desserts, I make sure to bring our own food as well. We make enough for everyone to share and it is always a great success. Everyone seems to love it and at the same time, they are introduced to a healthier way of eating.

Some might argue that their child will feel left out if they don't eat what everyone else is eating, and I couldn't disagree more. Your child is learning to value themselves and have confidence in their choices by having something only if they choose to and not because of peer pressure. This confidence will be with them even when faced with other temptations from peers as they get older. My obligation is to my children and making sure they have optimal nutrition, not in worrying if someone might get offended because I choose not to eat their cake. An easy way to get your child to want the healthy dessert you made is to let them help make it. When we have a birthday party to go to, I have my girls pick a cake they want to make, and we make it together. By the time of the party, they want to eat the cake that they helped to make.

Again, this varies with the age of the child. When they are young, they don't really know the effects of what some foods will do to their energy and bodies, so you're making that decision for them. But as they get older and learn more, they decide for themselves. As long as they feel listened to and respected and meals are typically enjoyable, they will make great choices later on, especially if it is modelled (not dictated) by the parents. And if they do choose to eat something you don't agree with, that's OK as well. Keep the focus on being together, creating conversations and connecting, rather than what's on the plate. Forget the guilt and shaming and just let them enjoy it!

INGREDIENTS

VARIATION:

Alternate your food. Not only does alternating give you the nutritional variety your body needs, but the habit also keeps you from developing a sensitivity or possible allergy to one kind of food. If you're having kale one day, have Swiss chard the next and so on.

FLEXIBILITY

The recipes in this book are really flexible – feel free to replace any sweetener, green or ingredient that is being used with something similar if it's not available to you.

SWEETENERS

"Historically, we ate the equivalent of only 20 teaspoons of sugar a year as a hunter/gatherer species. Now we eat 158 pounds per person per year, or about 50 teaspoons or half a pound each day. The average schoolboy has 34 teaspoons of sugar a day."[4]

A little much, don't you think? The effect this is having on our health and our children's health is pretty clear from more behavioral issues, tooth decay and an increase of diabetes and obesity. It's not that hard to see it when you add up breakfast cereals, fruit juices, processed granola (or 'health' bars), yogurts, flavored milk, soft drinks and candy bars. Not to mention, sugar is also in packaged foods, like crackers and condiments, to name a few. Advertisers do a great job of making us think this stuff is good for us! Nature has provided us with the best sweetness in life, and that's fruits. This is my main choice for sweetening up dessert. They work great, and the outcome is always a delicious blend. If a liquid sweetener is needed, then I use either honey, coconut nectar or maple syrup. If you want to avoid all 'sweet' foods but still want that 'sweet' flavor, stevia can be used.

Note: Although fruits are natural sugars, it is best to consume them in moderation as well, and if someone is sick or has an infection, you should completely avoid them until the person is healed. Dried fruit are highly concentrated in sweetness, so they're used only in desserts here. Fresh fruits are great on their own or chopped up in plain, unsweetened yogurt.

Fresh and dried fruits: Fruits are a real treasure. They contain vitamins, minerals and antioxidants. There are so many possibilities, from mangoes and peaches to banana and dates. Experiment with the different tastes and textures you're looking for. Dried fruit include dates, raisins, mulberries, apricots, gogi berries, figs, etc.

Stevia: Stevia is made from the leaves of the stevia plant. It has no calories and does not increase your blood sugar, which is why it is a great alternative for people who have diabetes, those that are on a candida diet or just can't have fruits for one reason or another. It is pretty sweet, so just a couple of drops is needed. When buying stevia, it is important to read the labels, as some stevia sold has added ingredients.

Maple syrup: Maple syrup is made from the sap of maple trees, which is then heated to evaporate most of the water, leaving the syrup. It is high in fructose and also contains some zinc and manganese. It has a unique flavor, and I use it in small quantities when a liquid sweetener is better for use.

Raw Honey: Oh, lovely honey! Honey is super sweet and my girls' favorite. If they could have it every day, they certainly would! It is great to use when someone has a cold or sore throat; making a honey/lemon/garlic/ginger drink always seems to soothe, as honey is antibacterial. Also, putting raw honey on a wound is helpful.

Coconut nectar: Coconut nectar comes from the liquid sap from coconut trees, it is low on the glycemic chart. So if you're watching your blood sugar levels, this is a much better choice to use when a liquid sweetener is needed in a recipe. It also contains some vitamins and minerals.

SUPERFOODS

I love superfoods. They are exceptionally nutritious and always give us a boost. They are great to add to smoothies or just to have on their own as a snack. There are tons of superfoods out there, and each one offers its own unique proprieties. It can get overwhelming at first, but just pick the ones that speak to you. According to David Wolfe, "by eating superfoods, you have more energy, you're more alert, your brain works better, you're more innovative, your ideas come quicker, your wit is sharper."[5] Like anything, though, it's good to alternate so that you're sure to have a variety. Below are some superfoods that we really enjoy along with some musts in our diets.

Bee pollen: Bee pollen is a complete food and has everything we need. It can be sprinkled on granola, pancakes or just eaten with a spoon.

Gogi berries: Gogi berries are super high in antioxidants and are also a complete protein. They also taste great; my kids love to snack on these. They taste amazing in the power biscotti recipe (page 57) or in a smoothie.

Spirulina: This is also a complete protein and has been known to be one of the best sources of protein in the world! It is an algae and is great added in smoothies or nut balls, as it doesn't have a strong taste.

Chlorella: This is very similar to spirulina in color and is also very high in protein. It's considered a whole food and is rich in minerals and vitamins.

Seaweed: Seaweed come from the ocean and have been a staple food in Asian diets. It contains vitamins, minerals and antioxidants. A little goes a long way! Different varieties of seaweed include: nori, kelp, dulse, kombu and wakame.

Sprouts: Sprouts are living foods and they can contain "up to 100 times more enzymes than raw fruits and vegetables, allowing your body to extract more vitamins, minerals, amino acids and essential fats from the foods you eat."[6] I am referring to leafy sprouts like broccoli, alfalfa, wheatgrass, red clover etc. Sprouts are also great because they can be grown right in your home at any time of year!

Essential Fatty Acids - Essential Fatty Acids, or EFAs, are types of fat that are essential in the diet because they can't be produced by the body. These fats help build cells, regulate the nervous system, strengthen the cardiovascular system, build immunity, and help the body absorb nutrients. EFAs are vital for healthy brain function. Omega rich foods include chia seeds, hemp & flax seeds and fish oils.

Fermented foods/probiotics: These are a must for keeping a healthy gut. According to Donna Gates author of *The Body Ecology Diet*, if you have a healthy gut you will have a strong immune system. Fermented foods include yogurts, coconut kefirs, miso, sauerkraut, and fermented veggies.

Bone Broth: "Bone broths made from chicken, fish or beef bones are a staple of the traditional food way of life. The storehouse of nutrients liberated from bone and connective tissues accelerates overall healing and supports our own bones, as well as teeth, joints, digestion and immunity. Properly prepared broth contains a generous amount of a wide range of minerals, such as calcium, magnesium, phosphorus and silica. Think of it as the ultimate multi-mineral "supplement." Since these naturally derived minerals are extracted from bone, they are in an ideal balance and easily utilized by the body."[7]

I make a weekly chicken broth and use the broth as a base for soups. I cook all my grains or legumes in the broth as well.

Recipe for Chicken bone broth:

Chicken bones	1 bay leaf
2 sticks of celery	Salt to taste
1 large onion	2 tbsp. apple cider vinegar
2-3 carrots	

Fill a large stock pot with water at ¾ level, add the bones and bring it to a boil on high heat. When it comes to a boil, remove the foamy parts that float to the top and lower the heat to medium. Add the vegetables and apple cider vinegar. Cook for about 12-24hrs.
Note: You need to keep adding water as necessary.

Celtic Sea Salt/Himalayan pink salt: These salts are high quality, they're not processed and no chemicals added to it. Because of this they contain all of the 84 live elements found in the ocean. In a recipe that calls for salt, any one of these can be used.

Oils: When referring to oils, I'm talking about using "extra virgin non-refined oils." My choices for cooking are coconut oil and olive oil. I also use hemp seed oil and flax seed oil only in its raw form.

SOAKING NUTS, SEEDS, BEANS & GRAINS

Most nuts, seeds, beans and grains contain phytic acid which blocks us from absorbing some vitamins and benefits from the foods we're eating. From the Weston A.Price Foundation "Phytic acid is the principal storage form of phosphorus in many plant tissues, especially the bran portion of grains and other seeds. It contains the mineral phosphorus tightly bound in a snowflake-like molecule. In humans and animals with one stomach, the phosphorus is not readily bioavailable. In addition to blocking phosphorus availability, the "arms" of the phytic acid molecule readily bind with other minerals, such as calcium, magnesium, iron and zinc, making them unavailable as well. In this form, the compound is referred to as phytate."[8]

Soaking the food beforehand, at least 8 hours helps to de-activate this. I soak it in water and a little bit of lemon. For nuts and seeds, I then dry them in the dehydrator, or an oven at the lowest temperature can also be used for drying of the nuts.

KITCHEN APPLIANCES USED:

High powered blender: I have the Vita-Mix
Food processor
Ice cream maker
Dehydrator
Juicer

RECITES

DRINKS

The thing that I see kids drink the most is juices. Juice boxes are big with kids but they're heated and filled with preservatives, not an ideal drink to have, not to mention all the added sugars. According to an article by Dr.Mercola, not from concentrate does not mean less processed:

"Generally speaking, whenever you buy a beverage that consistently tastes the same, you can be sure it's made using a patented recipe. And that recipe includes added flavors that may or may not fit the definition of natural."[9]

So what in the world will my kid drink? Well there are plenty of great fluids that will quench thirst and nourish you as well!

Of course, the number one drink is WATER! Having a good filter is a great investment as most tap water contains fluoride and chlorine.

If your family doesn't like the taste of plain water you can add a squeeze of lemon. Or throw in some berries and let it sit for about 30 minutes for the water to get the flavor.

If you're going to have juices then I suggest making your own. These juice recipes can also be put in popsicle molds to have as a nice cool treat when it's hot.

Red Ruby Lips

1 big beet (about 1½ cups)
5 sticks of celery
1 stick of fennel (with the leafy part as well)
½ English cucumber
¾ lime
Juice everything in the juicer.

Red Ruby Lips

Orange Juice

6 Oranges
1 celery stick
3 kale stems
Juice everything, I use the kale stems left over from making the kale chips.

Apple cucumber Juice

2 green apples
1 large English cucumber

Raspberry or Nettle tea

Boil a big pot of water, when it boils turn off the stove and add a couple tbsp. of dried nettle and/or raspberry leaves. Cover and let it sit. Strain out the herbs and enjoy! Both raspberry and nettle tea are rich in calcium, vitamins and minerals so I like to alternate between them.

NOTE: This can be done with any herbal plants that are safe for kids. Chamomile is a good one also for calming.

Nut Milks:

Nut milks are super easy to do and fast! All you need is a good blender, nut-milk bag, nuts, water and any other flavoring you might want to add. I like to keep them simple, especially if the milk is being used in a recipe. If you will be drinking it on its own then some dates can be added to give it some sweetness. Also, feel free to add a dash of vanilla or cinnamon to give it some flavor. You can make chocolate milk by adding either carob or some cacao.

The pulp can be made into a flour and used in recipes. It can be frozen and when it's needed for use, defrost, de-hydrate and grind it up into a flour. In a recipe that calls for almond flour, this is what it is.

Basic Recipe:

Almond milk

1 cup of almonds (soaked overnight)
4 cups of water

Blend all together and strain through a nut milk bag.

Coconut Drinks:

Coconut water is big here in our home, the best is from Thai young coconuts, they are so sweet, have electrolytes and there are many things you can do with them. You can drink the coconut water, make coconut water kefir, coconut milk, and coconut butter.

How to open a coconut:

Step 1. Use a machete or a big chopping knife to chop all around.

Step 2. Once shell is broken, take it off. Jelly might be exposed or it might be stuck to the shell.

Step 3. Under this piece of jelly is the tasty sweet water.

How to open a coconut

Coconut water

Open up a fresh coconut and enjoy!

Coconut Kefir

Step 1. Open a coconut, strain the water to make sure there is no husk.
Step 2. Warm the water up to room temperature, fill it in a mason jar and throw kefir grains inside.
Step 3. Cover with a cloth and leave it on your counter for 48hrs.
Step 4. When the jar is opened, strain out the kefir grains and use it for a new batch.
Step 5. If the kefir grains are not being used right away, put them in a Tupperware with water for a later use.

SMOOTHIES

Smoothies are great. They can be used as a meal, a snack, poured over cereals and it's a great way to get those leafy greens inside! The best combos that kids really go for generally include bananas, mango and berries. So experiment and see what flavors work best for you.

Tips to make your smoothie experience even more awesome!

- Rule of thumb is about 70% greens to 30% fruits, but if you're just starting go ahead and add fruit to your liking. Over time you can slowly phase out some of the fruit to make your smoothie more "green".

- Rotate your fruits and veggies, you get the nutritional value from a whole set of different produce and your body is less likely to develop a sensitivity to one type of food.

- All the recipes can be altered. Depending on your location and what time of the year it is, some ingredients might not be in season, so use what is available for you. You can always replace a leaf of kale with another leafy green. Here is a list of greens that work well in smoothies: Kale, spinach, collard greens, watercress, swiss chard, romaine lettuce, dandelion, mustard greens, bok choi, arugula, beet greens, celery

- A trick for those picky eaters who don't like anything that resembles the color of green slime is to add berries to the smoothie. First blend up all the greens and then add the berries last.

- I generally use water as a base in my smoothies, if you like your smoothie thick add less water and if you like it thin add more. This really goes according to your preference. Also any liquid like nut milks or coconut milk/water can replace the water to make it have more substance and be creamier.

Directions for making a smoothie: Blend all ingredients, adding the berries always last!

Creamy blueberry Smoothie

1 pear
1 banana
½ avocado
1 cup spinach
1 stick celery
2 cups frozen blueberries
Water

Blueberry Rush Smoothie

1 cup spinach
2 bananas
3 tbsp flax seeds
½ cup water
2 cups blueberries

Pear hemp smoothie

3 pears
1 banana
3 leaves romaine lettuce
2 tbsp hemp seeds
1 cup blueberries
Water

Mango-berry Smoothie

1 mango
1 banana
2 celery sticks
1 cup cucumbers
½ cup raspberry
Water

Raspberry Tart Smoothie

1 pear
3 leaves of kale
2 celery sticks
1½ cups blueberries
1 cup raspberry
1 tbsp. grounded flax seeds
Water

Mango Smoothie

4 leaves of chard
2 celery sticks
1 bunch parsley
2 mangoes
2 ½ bananas
Water

Zucchini rush Smoothie

3 sticks of celery
½ cup zucchini
1 tbsp alfalfa sprouts
1 tbsp grounded golden flax seeds

1 cup blueberries
1 cup raspberries
1 banana
Water

Blackberry Smoothie

2 packs blackberries (12oz)
3 leaves of bok choy
4 leaves of spinach
1 tbsp coconut oil
1 tbsp hemp seeds
2-3 drops of stevia
Water

Kiwilicious

4 kiwis
2 pears
2 leaves bok choi
½ cup hemp seeds
1 cup of water

Apple Cinnamon Smoothie

4 sticks of celery
2 apples
1 pear
½ tbsp. cinnamon powder

Kiwilicious

Simple Stawberry smoothie

2 ripe bananas
2 sticks of celery
1 cup fresh or frozen strawberries
1 tbsp. coconut butter (optional)

Gogi Berry Smoothie

3 bananas
3 leaves of swiss chard
1 tbsp. gogi berries

Pumpkin Spice 'Green' Smoothie

1 cup squash chopped
2 cups water
¼ cup pumpkin seeds
3 bananas
3 sticks of celery
1 tbsp. cinnamon
½ tsp. nutmeg
⅛ tsp. salt
Sprinkle of hemp seeds
Blend water and squash to make a puree, then add all the other ingredients and sprinkle with hemp seeds.

Hungry Hearty Man's Smoothie
This recipe comes from my husband!

1 cup oat groats
1 cup almonds
¼ cup hemp seeds
3 bananas
4 leaves of kale
4 cups of water
⅛ tsp. salt

Pumpkin Spice 'Green Smoothie'

BREAKFAST

You've all heard it, breakfast is the most important meal of the day! Our bodies fast all night while we're sleeping so it's no surprise by the time we wake up in the morning that we're usually hungry. A great whole foods meal starts us off right in the morning and gives us the energy we need to function at our best.

First thing in the morning after waking up, before eating anything, try starting off with a glass of water and a sprinkle of lemon. This flushes out toxins and balances our pH levels in the body.

At breakfast time, I know how rushed it can get in the morning and how easy it can be to grab a typical cereal box, although these are extremely fast and convenient, they're also loaded with artificial sugars and preservatives which will affect moods and attention span. Having a nourishing balanced breakfast provides us with the fuel, mental and physical energy we need for our day.

Another common breakfast meal is eggs. Soft or hard boiled eggs are a favorite, having them on homemade crackers topped with a leaf of lettuce is a great nutritious filling breakfast.

On a day where you have more time a "frittata" is packed with greens!

Frittata with Greens
Recipe from my mom! Maria Cavalieri D'Oro

4 leaves of kale (equal to 1½ cups of packed chopped kale)
½ bunch of spinach (equal to 3 cups of packed chopped spinach)
4 medium sized zucchinis (cut in 4 and then sliced in half centimeter)
1 large white onion
3 tbsp of olive oil
1 tsp. salt
2 tbsp. chopped parsley
2 tbsp. chopped basil
1 clove of garlic chopped
2 tbsp. chives
1 tbsp. chopped rosemary
½ tsp chili pepper

Need a 28cm pan with lid.

Step 1: With the burner on at medium high, add 2 tbsp. of olive oil, then add the zucchini and and cook for about 3 minutes stirring occasionally.

Step 2: Add sliced onions and ½ tsp. of salt. Stir all together. After a few minutes add all the herbs, stir all together, cover and let simmer for about 4 to 5 minutes stirring occasionally.

Step 3: Add all the leafy greens and sprinkle with the remaining ½ tsp. of salt and cover until the leaves have shrinked to half. Stir all, cover and cook stirring occasionally for about another 5 to 8 minutes.

Step 4: Slightly beat the 4 eggs. Add eggs to pan and stir making sure to pat the frittata down evenly.

Step 5: Lower the heat a drop more and let the frittata cook for about 4 to 5 minutes shaking the pan occasionally to make sure the bottom doesn't stick to the pan.

Step 6: Place a dish slightly bigger over the pan and turn over the frittata.

Step 7: Scrape the pan and add the last tablespoon of olive oil. Return the other side of the frittata back in the pan and pat down evenly. Cook for another 4 to 5 minutes moving the pan to make sure it doesn't stick to the bottom.

Frittata with Greens

Apple Cinnamon Granola

3 cups soaked and sprouted buckwheat
1 cup sunflowers (soaked)
1 cup walnuts (soaked)
½ cup pumpkin seeds
4 tbsp coconut oil
½ cup dates (about 8-9)

1 apple
1 cup raisins
1 tsp spirulina (or any other green powder)
1½ tbsp. cinnamon
½ tsp nutmeg
⅛ tsp salt

Step 1: Soak and sprout buckwheat. Soak buckwheat overnight, then strain out the water and cover it with a cloth, leave it on your counter for about 2-3 days for it to sprout. Note: Rinse the buckwheat twice daily morning and evening.

Step 2: When the buckwheat is ready, in a food processor combine the coconut oil with dates, apple, raisins and spices until it comes like a paste.

Step 3: In a coffee grinder, pulse the walnuts, sunflower and pumpkin seeds to desired consistency.

Step 4: Mix everything together by hand, buckwheat, paste and nuts. Making sure to massage the paste everywhere.

Step 5: Dehydrate at 115 until it's crispy. If you don't have a dehydrator you can bake it at the lowest temperature in the oven.

Apple Cinnamon Granola

Breakfast cereal with sauce

2 cups ground walnuts (pecans or almonds)
1 big juicy ripe pear
1 leaf of bok choy
2 tbsp of coconut butter

Grind the walnuts up and place in a bowl. Blend up all the other ingredients and when smooth pour it over the walnuts. You can also top the cereals with one of your favorite green smoothies!

Breakfast Pie

Crust:
2 cups pecans
2 leaves of baby bok choi (about ⅓ cup)
1 tbsp raw honey
Process everything and flatten out in a mini dish.

Filing:
2 pears
2 tbsp sauerkraut
1 tbsp coconut butter

Blend everything in a high speed blender. Pour over the crust and sprinkle it with cinnamon.

Breakfast Pie

Gluten/egg free Pancakes

Gluten/egg free Pancakes

1 cup millet flour (brown rice flour can be used as well)
½ tbsp. aluminum free baking soda
1 tbsp. cinnamon (1½ cinnamon sticks)
1 tsp. nutmeg

1 Fiji apple (or add a banana for a sweeter taste)
2 leaves of Swiss chard
1 cup water (for a richer consistency use coconut milk)
⅛ tsp. Celtic sea salt

In a blender, add chopped up apples and greens, then the dry ingredients, and lastly the water. Blend on high until smooth.
Blending it this way forms less clumps at the bottom. If dry ingredients get stuck to the side of the blender, with a spatula wipe it up and re-blend.
Lightly oil a pan with coconut oil and cook on medium heat, flipping it on the other side when the sides of the pancakes start to release.
Variations: Mix the batter with some chopped fruits.
Serve with some blueberry jam, smoothie, a nut butter or a nut spread.

Zucchini/avocado Spread

1 avocado
½ cup zucchini
½ hemp seeds
1 tsp flax seeds
3 tbsp carob powder
6 dates
⅛ tsp salt
1 tbsp coconut oil

Process everything in the food processor.

Nut Spread

¾ cup almonds
½ cup hazelnuts
¼ cup pumpkin seeds
½ tsp salt
¼ cup carob powder
½ cup swiss chard (1 big leaf)
6 dates
2 tbsp. coconut oil
⅛ cup of water

Process everything in the processor, add more water if needed for desired consistency.

Almond butter

2 cups almond butter

I make my almond butter in the processor, put the almonds in and process, stopping every once and a while to clear sides until it gets smooth. NOTE: Make sure you have a strong processor or it might overheat. Almond butter can also be done in a high speed blender.

Oatmeal

1½ cups gluten free rolled oats
1 banana
½ apple
1 tbsp. chia seeds
1 tbsp. cinnamon powder
1 tbsp. of green powder (chlorella, spirulina, etc.)
⅛ tsp. salt

Directions: Grind everything together in the food processor until it is smooth. YES it's as simple as that! When it hardens you can roll it into balls or a bar and pack it up for a snack.

Chia Porridge

1½ soaked chia
⅓ cup coconut flakes
⅓ cup hemp seeds
2 tbsp cinnamon
1 apple cut up into pieces
⅛ salt
½ tsp vanilla powder
¼ tsp clove powder
1½ banana
2 dates
2 leaves of chard

Process the banana, dates and Swiss chard in the processor until it is like a cream. Mix all the other ingredients in a bowl, when it is all combined add the cream mixture and mix well. Serve and enjoy!

Chia Porridge

Mango Porridge

4 leaves of baby bok choi
2 mangoes
2 cups chia gel
½ cup coconut flakes
1-2 dates or a couple drops of stevia

Blend everything in blender and top with chopped mangoes

Mango Porridge

Chia Gel
1 part chia to 6 part water
Put chia seeds first, then add the water on top, stir (so it doesn't become 1 big lump).
Refrigerate overnight – Lasts about 2-3 days in the fridge.

DIPS & CRACKERS

Cut up a plate of raw veggies, put them on the table with a delicious dip and watch them disappear! They're also great just spread on a homemade cracker for lunch or a snack. Crackers are also great for breakfast with any one of the spreads or a nut butter. I also pack them up when I know we'll be out for a while as a snack with a fruit.

Squash Dip

2 cups diced squash   1 tbsp. tahini
1 clove garlic (¼ tsp)   ¼ tsp salt
½ cup of bok choy   1 tbsp. flax seed oil

Steam the squash, when it is soft and cooled a bit, throw everything in a high speed blender until smooth. Great dip for crudités or to spread on romaine lettuce.

Squash Dip

Zucchini Hummus

2 zucchini (about 2 cups)
½ tsp garlic (2 small cloves)
1 tbsp. chopped parsley
2 tbsp. tahini
½ tsp salt
1 tbsp. juice of a lime
2 tbsp. olive oil
2 tsp. sun dried tomatoes

Peel zucchini, and put everything in the blender or food processor until smooth.

Zucchini Hummus
Photo credit: Seta Soukiassian

Chickpea Hummus

2 cups cooked chickpeas (cooked in chicken broth)
1 clove garlic – about ½ tsp chopped
1 celery stick
¼ cup tahini
¼ cup olive oil
½ cup water
¼ tsp salt
¼ tsp kelp powder

Blend everything in the blender until smooth. Add more water if needed.

Chickpea Hummus
Photo credit: Thea Barbato

Summer Garden Crackers

2 tbsp. fresh rosemary
1 cup basil
¼ cup fresh parsley
2 tbsp. leafy part of fennel
¼ cup dandelion
½ tsp salt
1½ cup ground pumpkin seeds
1 tbsp. olive oil

In a food processor combine all the ingredients except the pumpkin seeds and olive oil. Then in a bowl combine the grounded pumpkin seeds, olive oil and the greens until well combined. Roll it flat with a rolling pin and cut it in desired shapes. Place on an oiled baking sheet and bake at 300 for 10-15 minutes, then flip them over and bake for another 5 minutes.

Summer Garden Crackers

Broccoli Crackers

2 cups pumpkin seeds
1 cup shredded broccoli
1 tsp. dried basil
1 tsp. rosemary
½ tsp. salt
1 tbsp. extra virgin olive oil

Grind up the pumpkin seeds into a powder and set aside. Process the broccoli fine. In a mixing bowl mix the ground pumpkin seeds, broccoli, spices, salt and oil until well combined. Roll it flat with a rolling pin and cut it in desired shapes. Place on an oiled baking sheet and bake at 300 for 10-15 minutes, then flip it on the other side and bake it for another 10-15 minutes. Depending how crispy you like them!

Broccoli Crackers

Thyme onion cracker

2 cups ground sunflower seed
1½ cup ground flax seeds
2 cloves garlic
1 cup kale
1 tbsp. fresh thyme
⅛ cup sunflower seed oil
½ onion
¼ tsp salt

In a food processor combine garlic, kale, thyme, onion and salt. Then in a bowl combine the grounded sunflower seeds, grounded flax seeds, olive oil and the greens until well combined. Roll it flat with a rolling pin and place on a teflex sheet in the dehydrator. Dehydrate at 115 for 6 hours, then flip them over and put them directly on the mesh. Dehydrate for another couple of hours until it reaches your desired crispiness.

MAIN MEALS

Our main meals always contains a green whether it's as a side dish or in the main meal itself. Examples: Baked chicken with steamed or raw broccoli, salmon with beets and a salad

These meals are great if you have someone that doesn't mind eating greens on their own, but for someone that REALLY resists eating anything green then a great option is to add them in burgers or patties.

Kids love noodles as well, I stay away from the gluten filled noodles and tend to get either a brown rice jasmine noodle or mung bean noodles, Mix it up and use different sauces and veggies each time.

Black bean nori wrap

1 cup cooked blacked beans   Nori sheets
Zucchini hummus   Lettuce

On a nori sheet, spread a layer of zucchini hummus, add some black beans and lettuce. Roll up and enjoy!

Lentil Stew

1 cup chopped leeks   2 cloves of garlic
1 celery stick   1-2 tsp salt (depending if using broth or not)
¼ cup fennel   2 leaves of swiss chard
4 ½ cups lentils   Drop of coconut oil
7 cups of bone broth (or water)

In a pan, heat the coconut oil, add the leeks, celery and fennel until it is all combined and the veggies start to get a little soft.

Add the lentils and mix everything so it is well combined. Then add the water and bring to a boil. When it boils add the salt and the garlic cloves. Lower the heat to medium and cook for about half an hour.

In the meantime, process the swiss chard in the food processor so it is finely chopped. Add it in the lentil pot about 10 minutes before the lentils are ready.

Chick Pea Spinach patties

1 leaf of bok choi
3 tbsp. chopped yellow pepper
⅓ cup onion
2 tbsp. chopped parsley
1 cup spinach
2 cups cooked chick peas
¼ tsp salt
½ tbsp. apple cider vinegar
1 cup cooked millet
1 tbsp. ground flax seeds
Drop of coconut oil

Process all ingredients except millet and flax seeds in a food processor. Transfer to a bowl and stir in the millet and flax seeds. Form in patties shape and place on parchment paper lined with coconut oil. Bake at 350 for 15 minutes on one side, then turn sides and bake for another 15 minutes.

Chick Pea Spinach patties

Raw Pad Thai

Recipe by Sarah Phipp <u>www.nutsabouthealth.co.uk</u>
Equipment needed: blender or food processor

2 medium to large courgette (zucchini)
2 medium to large carrots
2 cups mung bean sprouts
100g or ¾ cup chopped nuts (use almonds or cashews)
1 red or yellow pepper, sliced into thin strips
4 spring onions, diced
½ cup fresh chopped coriander (cilantro)

For the dressing:
2 tbsp. almond butter
zest of 1 lime
2 tbsp. liquid aminos
juice from 2 limes
1 to 2 tbsp. chili flakes
1 tbsp. maple syrup
2 cloves fresh garlic, minced
1 tsp fresh ginger
1 tbsp cold-pressed olive oil
1 fresh red chili, (optional)

Using either a vegetable peeler or a spiraliser process the carrots and courgette (zucchini) into long strips.

Place the strips of courgette, carrot, onion, bean sprouts and pepper and chopped nuts together in a large bowl and mix well, just use your hands if you don't mind getting messy.

Place all the dressing ingredients into your food processor or blender and mix until all of it is liquidized.

Pour dressing over Pad Thai vegetables and then sprinkle over the chopped coriander. Slice the fresh chili finely then sprinkle over the top if desired.

Fettuccini con Tuna

½ cup dandelion

½ cup bok choi (1 big leaf)

1 Jerusalem artichoke (2 tbsp.)

A pack of brown Jasmine rice noodles

Drizzle of lemon

Drizzle of extra virgin olive oil

Celtic sea salt

A can of Tuna

1 zucchini

Step 1. Take zucchini and slice it with a mandolin slicer, set aside. Bring a pot to boil, when boils add salt and throw in the noodles. Cook according to package instructions.

Step 2. In the meantime, process the dandelion, bok choi and Jerusalem artichoke in the food processor until finely chopped.

Step 3. When noodles are ready, strain them and put them in a bowl. Add the veggie mixture, a can of Tuna and combine everything well. Add a sprinkle of lemon juice and drizzle with some olive oil and mix again.

When serving you can sprinkle some dulse flakes or nutritional yeast flakes (for a cheesy flavor) on top as well.

Fettuccini con Tuna

Sardine Patties

1 can of sardines (tuna can be used as well)   1 leaf of bok choy (about ½ cup)
1 stick of celery   ⅛ tsp salt
2 tbsp. fresh Italian parsley

Process everything in the food processor, when it is well combined form it into patties and place on an oiled baking sheet lined with parchment paper. Cover with aluminum foil. Bake at 350 for 10 minutes, uncover and flip the patties and bake for another 10 minutes.

Fish Patties

1 stick of celery   ½ tsp. fresh rosemary
1 cup of cabbage   3 large pieces of sole (about 3 cups)
4-6 leaves of basil (1 tbsp. finely chopped)   1 tsp. Celtic sea salt
1 tbsp. fresh parsley

Process everything in the food processor. Shape into patties and place on an oiled pan. Bake at 400 for 10 minutes, then flip sides and bake for another 5 minutes.

Fish Patties

Chicken Burgers

2 raw chicken breasts
5 grape tomatoes
2 leaves of kale
A handful of fresh basil leaves
1 cup cauliflower
1 tsp. celtic sea salt

Directions: Preheat oven at 375. Process everything into the food processor until it's all well combined. Oil a pan lined with parchment paper, shape batter into "burger" forms. Cook for 10 minutes on one side, then turn them over and cook for another 10 minutes.

Serve with Nori sheets, kale or collard leaves to make it as a wrap. Put any condiments you like in there as well, olives, tomatoes, lettuce, sauerkraut etc.

Chicken Burgers

SIDE DISHES, SAUCES & EXTRAS

Vegetable Salad
Recipe by Maria Cavalieri D'Oro

1 large eggplant
3 medium size zucchini
1 bunch of rapini
1 clove garlic
1 tbsp. parsley
1 tbsp. basil

Pinch of chili pepper
Salt to taste
1 tbsp. extra virgin olive oil
For dressing either balsamic vinegar or lemon and extra virgin olive oil.

Step 1. Wash the eggplant and zucchini and wrap them in aluminum foil.

Step 2. Place in oven at 425 degrees for about 1 hour turning the vegetables halfway through.

Step 3. Remove eggplant from oven and open the aluminum paper to let them cool down.

Step 4. In the meantime wash and cut your rapini. In a large pan add 1 tablespoon of olive oil, the garlic cut in 2 pieces and chili pepper. When oil is warm add the rapini, sprinkle them with salt, turn them and lower the heat between medium and high.

Cover the pan and cook, stirring occasionally for approximately 5 to 7 minutes or until done. If the pan dries out add a bit of water. Remove from pan and set aside.

Step 5. Once vegetables are cooled down open the eggplant and with a spoon discard most

Vegetable Salad

of its seeds, then cut eggplant in large chunks. Do the same with the zucchinis discard any large seeds and cut in large chunks also. Cut the rapini up in bite size portions.

Step 6. Mix all the vegetables together and add the parsley, basil and chopped garlic to your taste.

Stir all together and season with a bit of olive oil and either balsamic vinegar or lemon. Excellent warm or cold!

Cauliflower Mash

1 whole cauliflower
1 stick of fennel (about ½ cup)
1 clove of garlic
1 onion chive
½ cup of fresh basil
¼ cup red pepper
¼ tsp. salt
¼ tsp. kelp
Juice of ½ lemon
1 tbsp. hemp seed oil

Cauliflower Mash

Directions: Lightly steam the cauliflower (until you can put a fork in it), when it's ready and cooled down a little bit, add the cauliflower and all the other ingredients into the food processor and process until smooth.

Leek Soup

1 cup leek
½ cauliflower (about 2 cups)
1 leaf of collard
2 cups pumpkin

2 tbsp. parsley
3-4 cups chicken broth (or water)
Salt & Pepper to taste

Bring the broth or water to a boil, add all the other ingredients and simmer at medium for 20 minutes.

Tomato Sauce

7-8 fresh tomatoes
1 carrot
1 small onion
1 clove garlic

¼ cup fennel
Salt to taste
Olive oil

Directions: In a food processor, process the tomatoes, carrot, garlic and fennel. Set aside.

Oil a pot with olive oil and sauté the onion, then add the sauce and bring it to a boil. When it boils, add the salt and let it simmer at medium heat for about 30 minutes.

Leek and Butternut Squash Sauce

2 cups cubed leeks
2 cups cubed butternut squash
1 tablespoon of olive oil
1½ cups water
1 tablespoon of fresh combined parsley and basil or any other herbs of your choice
Salt and pepper
A few sprinkle of chili pepper to taste (optional)

In a pan put the tablespoon of olive oil. Add the cubed leeks and sauté for a few minutes.

Next add the cubed butternut squash and continue to simmer for a few minutes.
At this time add the water with the herbs, salt and pepper.

Lower the heat, cover and let simmer for about 20 minutes or until the sauce reaches the consistency desired.

Rappini

1 pack of rappini
1 tbsp. olive oil
1 tsp chopped garlic (about 2 cloves)

¼ tsp chili pepper
Salt to taste
Water

Sautee olive oil in pan with garlic and chili pepper for about a minute. Place rappini and salt in pan and stir it until it is well combined. Cover and lower heat to less than medium. Leave for about 2 minutes.

Kale Chips

3-4 packs of kale
Olive oil
Lemon juice
Celtic sea salt

De-stem the kale, wash and dry it. Massage the oil, lemon juice and salt on the kale leaves. Dehydrate at 115 until crispy, about 24 hours.

EXTRAS

These don't necessarily contain tons of greens but it's a couple of the 'standard' favorite made in a healthier version.

Replacing regular "french fries" with either squash or sweet potato fries.

Squash Fries

1 butternut squash
Pinch of celtic sea salt
Pinch black pepper
½ tbsp. olive oil

Cut the squash in strips, add the spices and oil and massage everything together until all the strips are well coated. On a baking pan, place some parchment paper on it and oil it. Then place squash on it and bake for 15-20 minutes at 350.

Squash Fries

Sweet Potato Fries

Sweet potatoes
Olive oil
Salt
Parsley
Basil

Directions: Preheat the oven to 425. Cut up some sweet potatoes in "fries" shape. Place them in a bowl and add a drop of olive oil and a sprinkle of salt.

Massage everything in. On a baking pan, place some parchment paper on it and oil it. Place the potatoes on it, then sprinkle some basil and parsley all over them.

Sweet Potato Fries

Bake for 15-20 minutes, then turn them on the other side and bake for another 15 minutes.

Gluten Free Bread Crumb Mix

1 cup gluten free oats (ground)   1 tsp. chopped parsley
½ cup golden flax seeds (ground)   1 tsp. chopped basil
1 clove of garlic minced   Pinch of salt

Mix everything together. For a cheesy flavor you can add some nutritional yeast flakes in the mix. This is a great recipe to have as a substitute for when you need 'breadcrumbs' in a recipe. You can do a big batch and store it in the freezer.

Chicken cutlets

Organic chicken breast
Olive oil
Breadcrumb mix

Slice the chicken breast in cutlets. Have 2 plates ready, one with the olive oil and one with the breadcrumb mixture. Dip the cutlets first in the oil and then bread it with the breadcrumb mixture. Place on a pan lined with parchment paper. Bake at 350 for 15 minutes on one side, then flip them over and bake for another 10 minutes.

Cut the chicken up smaller and you have chicken nuggets!

Chicken cutlets

DESSERTS

Desserts can be healthy and one of the best ways to get those greens in, especially if you have a really *picky* eater! They're sweet and it's really easy to mask the color. My choices of sweeteners are usually fruit and if a liquid is needed then I might use raw honey, coconut nectar or maple syrup. (See sweet section for more details). I've included a lot of recipes here because most kids eat a lot of sweets and I want to show you how easy it is to include greens in them!

Frozen Treats

On a hot summer day, there's nothing more refreshing than something cool like ice cream or sorbet. Having a good ice cream maker is definitely worth it! If a recipe calls for it and you don't have an ice cream maker you can put the ice cream in the freezer and keep stirring it up every half an hour until it's at your desired consistency.

In recipes that have vanilla beans you can substitute with pure ground vanilla powder.
1 vanilla bean = 1 tsp. vanilla powder

Krypto vanilla ice cream

2 cups almond milk
1 avocado
1 vanilla bean (1 tsp. vanilla powder)
2-3 bananas

⅛ tsp salt
1 leaf of swiss chard

Blend everything together in a high speed blender. When smooth, put it in the ice cream maker and follow directions.

Coconut Cinnamon Ice cream

2 cups cashews
1½ cups of coconut milk
1 leaf collard greens
1 stick of celery
½ cup maple syrup
1 tbsp. cinnamon powder

Coconut Cinnamon Ice cream

Blend everything together in a high speed blender. When smooth, put it in the ice cream maker and follow directions.

Carob ice cream

2 cups cashews
2 ½ cups almond milk
1 vanilla bean or ½ tbsp. vanilla powder
10 dates
¼ cup carob
⅛ tsp salt
2 small leaves of kale (about ⅓ cup tightly packed)

Blend everything together in a high speed blender. When smooth, put it in the ice cream maker and follow directions.

Carob ice cream

Lemon Granita

1 big leaf of cabbage (about ½ cup)
2 cups water
½ cup coconut nectar (or any other liquid sweetener)

Zest of 1 lemon
Juice of 2 large lemons

Blend cabbage, coconut nectar and water first, then add the lemon juice and lemon zest. When well combined, pour in ice cube trays and put it in the freezer. When frozen, put in the food processor and pulse until desired consistency. Enjoy right away.

Variations: You can also do this in the ice cream maker.

Strawberry Sorbet

Strawberry Sorbet

½ cup baby bok choi
½ cup water
½ cup dried apricots
3 cups frozen strawberry

Blend the water, bok choi and apricots first, then slowly add in the frozen strawberries.

Enjoy right away or put it in the freezer for a couple of minutes to firm up a little bit more.

Cakes

Raw cakes are easy to make and you can always taste the result as you make it. No need to wait until it comes out of the oven to see if it tastes good. For special occasions we always whip one of these up and they're a great success!

Strawberry Chocolate Vanilla Cake

Cake:
2 cups walnut
1 cup dates (10-12)
1 cup pumpkin seeds
⅛ tsp salt
2 leaves of kale
Inside of 1 scrapped vanilla bean
½ cup carob powder

Frosting:
3 bananas
⅓ cup coconut flakes
⅓ cup coconut oil
1 tsp vanilla powder
1 tbsp coconut butter

Extra:
1 pack of strawberries

Directions:
Cake: Process the nuts, salt, kale, vanilla and carob powder. When it's all well combined add the dates. When it's all set, form it into 2 layers. Set aside.

Frosting: Blend everything in a blender. When smooth, put it in the fridge to harden a bit for about 10-15 minutes.

When the frosting is ready, frost one of the cake layers. Add some of the chopped up strawberries and then add the other cake layer on top. Frost all the rest. Decorate with the remaining strawberries.

Strawberry Chocolate Vanilla Cake

RAW mini zucchini cakes

4 cups shredded zucchini	**Filling**
1½ cup coconut flakes	2 cups cashews
1½ cups almond flour	2 cups coconut milk
1 cup walnuts (chopped up)	½ cup coconut nectar (or any other liquid
1 cup of dates	sweetener)
2 tbsp. cinnamon	2 tsp lemon juice
¼ tsp. salt	3 tbsp lime juice
½ tsp. clove	½ vanilla bean
¼ tsp. nutmeg	⅛ tsp salt
	1¼ cup coconut oil

Cake: Make your dates into a paste with a mortar and pestle or in the food processor. With a mixer, mix all the ingredients until everything is well combined. Form it into little cakes and dehydrate at 115 for a couple of hours to firm it up a bit.

Filling: Blend all ingredients in a high speed blender adding the coconut oil last. Put the filling in the freezer until it is firm (not frozen).

Assembly: Spread the filling on top of a cake, then add another cake layer on top.

RAW mini zucchini cakes

RAW CHEESECAKES

Raw cheesecakes are pretty standard with a nut based crust and a cashew filling (which is what give it a cheesy taste), but I found bananas was a good replacement for when I didn't want to use cashews, the only thing is you need to add more coconut butter if the filling is only fruit based. There's so many different combinations of nuts, fruits, greens and spices that you can use, here are some of our favorites!

Rasp-bana cheesecake Delight

Crust
2 cups pecans
8 medjool dates
½ cup spinach
¼ cup raw cacao
1/16 tsp salt

Directions: Process everything in the food processor until the mixture sticks together when you press it with your hands. Oil a spring form pan with coconut oil, then press the crust into the bottom of the pan.

Filling:
2 cups soaked cashews
1½ cup almond milk
1½ cup bananas (about 3)
1 cup raspberries
2 tbsp. lemon juice (about 1 lemon)
1½ tsp. lime juice
⅛ tsp. salt
1 cup coconut oil
2 tbsp. coconut butter

Blend all ingredients except the coconut oil & butter. When all ingredients are well combined, add the coconut oil and coconut butter. Blend again until it is smooth. Pour filling over crust and freeze until it is firm but not frozen (about 3-4 hours). When firm put it in the fridge. When ready to serve, take it out of the spring form pan and decorate to your liking with raspberries and a chocolate icing.

Choco Spice raw cheesecake

Crust
2 cups walnuts
½ cup hemp seeds
9-10 medjool dates
1 tsp. chlorella
1/16 tsp. salt
½ cup carob powder

Directions: Process everything in the food processor until the mixture sticks together when you press it with your hands. Oil a spring form pan with coconut oil, then press the crust into the bottom of the pan.

Filling
2¾ cups soaked cashews
2 cups almond milk
½ cup kale (about 3 leaves)
3 tbsp. lemon juice
½ cup maple syrup (or any other liquid sweetener)
2 tbsp. cinnamon powder
4 tbsp. carob powder
⅛ tsp. salt
1 cup of melted coconut oil
2 tbsp. coconut butter

Blend the cashew, almond milk, kale, lemon juice, maple syrup and salt. When it's well combined, add the cinnamon and carob powder. Then add the coconut oil last. When it's smooth pour it over the crust and freeze it until it gets firm (about 3-4 hours).

When it's firm put it in the fridge and when ready to serve, take it out of the spring form pan and decorate to your liking.

Nanna's Blueberry Cheesecake Crust

2 cups pecans
½ cup hemp seeds
⅓ cup carob powder
½ cup baby bok choi
1/16 tsp salt
7-8 dates

Directions: Process everything in the food processor until the mixture sticks together when you press it with your hands. Oil a spring form pan with coconut oil, then press the crust into the bottom of the pan.

Filling
2 cups cashews
2 leaves chard (½ cup)
¾ cup hemp seed milk
3 ½ cup fresh blueberries
2 bananas
1½ tsp lime juice
1/16 tsp salt
1 cup melted coconut oil
2 tbsp. coconut butter

Blend all ingredients except the coconut oil. When all ingredients are well combined, add the coconut oil. Blend again until it is smooth.

Pour filling over crust and freeze until it is firm but not frozen (about 3-4 hours). When firm put it in the fridge. When ready to serve, take it out of the spring form pan and decorate to your liking with some fresh blueberries.

Strawberry Cheesecake

Crust

2 cups pecans

1 leaf of collard greens (½ cup)

5-6 dates (½ cup)

¼ tsp vanilla powder

Directions: Process everything in the food processor until the mixture sticks together when you press it with your hands. Oil a spring form pan with coconut oil, then press the crust into the bottom of the pan.

Filling

3 bananas

1 pack strawberries (3 cups)

½ tsp. vanilla powder

1 cup coconut oil

4 tbsp. coconut butter

Blend all ingredients except the coconut oil and coconut butter. When all ingredients are well combined, add the coconut oil & butter. Blend again until it is smooth.

Pour filling over crust and freeze until it is firm but not frozen (about 3-4 hours). When firm put it in the fridge. When ready to serve, take it out of the spring form pan and decorate to your liking with some fresh strawberries.

Strawberry Cheesecake

Pecan Pear Pie

Crust
3 cups of pecans
1 leaf of collard greens
1 tbsp. cinnamon
2 tbsp. raw honey

Crust: Process everything in the food processor, line a pie dish with saran wrap and put the crust inside. Place in the dehydrator for about 4-6 hrs. Remove the pie crust from the plate and place in the dehydrator until the crust is firm.

Filling
2 pears
½ apple
2 tbsp lemon juice
4 tbsp. coconut butter
Blend everything until smooth.

Assembly: Once the crust is ready, put it back in the pie dish and add the filling on top. Decorate with sliced pear or apples and sprinkle with cinnamon.

These icings are great to decorate and to write on the cakes.

Chocolate Icing
1 banana
½ cup coconut oil
½ cup raw cacao

1 tsp spirulina
1 tbsp cup coconut butter

Blend everything up until smooth. Place the icing in a pastry bag and decorate to your liking. Variation: you can just use this as a dip for fruits!

Carob Icing
2 bananas
¼ cup spinach

⅓ cup carob powder
⅓ cup coconut oil

Blend everything up until smooth. Place the icing in a pastry bag and decorate to your liking. Variation: you can just use this as a dip for fruits!

COOKIES, ENERGY BALLS, CHOCOLATES & PUDDINGS

Power Biscotti

½ cup almonds
1 cup almond flour
½ cup coconut flakes
½ cup spinach
Rind of 1 lemon

Juice of 1 lemon
½ cup gogi berries
½ cup mulberries
½ cup of dried apricots

Combine everything except the lemon rind/juice in the processor and process until well combined. Transfer to a bowl and add the lemon juice and rind, mix by hand. Form into 2 loaves and put to dehydrate on the mesh at 115 for 3 hours. Take out and cut in desired length and put back to dehydrate for another 5 hours or until desired crispiness.

Power Biscotti

Chocolate Chip Cookies

4 cups almond flour (leftover pulp from almond milk)
¾ cups golden flax seeds
1 tsp. vanilla powder
¼ tsp. salt
1 leaf of collard
2 bananas
2 tbsp. maple syrup
Chocolate chips (see recipe 'Chocolate without the caffeine')

Directions: mix all dry ingredients in a bowl. Set aside. In a blender, blend the bananas, collard greens and maple syrup. Add the wet mixture to the dry mixture and combine it all together by hand. Form into cookie shapes and dehydrate at 115 until desired consistency (usually about 20-24 hrs). These can also be baked at 375 for 10-15 minutes.

Chocolate Chip Cookies

Hazelnut Balls

Chocolate Crispy Balls

3 cups pecans
2/3 cups hemp seeds
½ cup carob powder
2 tsp. stevia
⅛ tsp. salt
2 tbsp. coconut oil
½ cup fresh spinach
a handful of puffed millet

Process everything in the food processor except the puffed millet. When the batter is sticky and can easily be formed into balls, transfer mixture to a bowl and add the puffed millet. Mix by hand and form into balls.

Hazelnut Balls

2 cups hazelnut
2/3 cup hemp seeds
1 leaf of kale

1 cup medjool dates
½ cup raw carob powder

Process all ingredients in the food processor until it is sticky enough to form it into balls. Shape into balls and roll in coconut flakes.
It can also be rolled in carob powder or hemp seeds.

Cinnamon balls

1 cup almonds
½ cup hemp seeds
1 leaf of bok choi
½ cup of raisins
1½ tbsp. of cinnamon

Directions: Process everything into the food processor until it is all sticky. Form into balls and roll it in some cinnamon.

Cinnamon balls

Chocolate

Making your own chocolate takes less than 10 minutes and the taste and purity of real cacao gives you a real boost. In making chocolate and adding greens it is best to use a powdered green if you're using the food processor. The cacao can be replaced with carob, when this will be for kids I use carob as it's not a stimulant and won't keep them up all night!

Note: Since I am using coconut butter instead of cacao butter the mixture is a little bit clumpier when working with.

Chocolate Delight!

½ cup cacao   2 ½ tbsp. maple syrup
½ cup carob   ½ cup coconut oil (melted)
2 tbsp fennel (the leafy part)   2 tbsp coconut butter (melted)

Process everything and put in chocolate molds. Refrigerate until hard.

Chocolate Delight!

Chewy Choco-berries

¼ cup melted coconut butter
¼ cup coconut oil
⅓ cup carob powder

2 tbsp cacao powder
½ tbsp. spirulina
½ cup mulberries

Process everything together and put in chocolate molds.

Chewy Choco-berries

Chocolate without the caffeine

¼ cup swiss chard (the leafy part)
½ cup of melted coconut oil
½ cup of medjool dates (about 5)

½ cup carob powder
1 cup of melted coconut butter

Blend the swiss chard, coconut oil and dates in a high speed blender, when it is well combined add the carob powder and melted coconut butter. Keep mixing it in the blender or if it's too hard you can do it by hand. When everything is well combined, place it in chocolate molds and refrigerate for about 1 hour. You can also shape these in little forms as chocolate chips.

Dark Maca chocolate (for adults only!)

½ cup raw cacao
2 tbsp cinnamon powder
1 tsp. chlorella
6 dates
4 tbsp coconut oil
1 tbsp. maca powder

Process everything in a food processor and place it flat in a pan. Put it in the freezer to harden for a couple of minutes. Take it out of the pan and cut into pieces.
A nice boost for us parents!

Dark Maca chocolate (for adults only!)

Pudding

Spiced Coconut pudding

2 cups of chia gel (see below for chia gel recipe)
1 coconut (flesh and water)
2 tbsp. cinnamon
½ tbsp. nutmeg
½ tbsp. cardamom
½ tsp. salt
2 leaves of kale
Stevia to taste (12-15 drops)

Blend everything together until smooth.

Creamy Carob pudding

1 medium size avocado
8 dates soaked in ¾ cup water
½ cup raw carob powder
2 cups almond milk
½ of one vanilla bean
⅛ tsp salt
1 leaf of swiss chard
4 tbsp chia seeds

Blend everything together in blender except chia seeds. Once blended, transfer to a bowl and stir in the chia seeds and refrigerate overnight. If you prefer a completely smooth pudding blend in the chia seeds with all ingredients.

Easy chocolate pudding

2 bananas
1 avocado
⅓ cup carob powder
¼ cup ground sesame seeds
1 cup of spinach

Process everything in the processor until smooth.

Easy chocolate pudding
Photo credit: Douglas A. Metzger

ENDNOTES

1 ''A spotlight on children's health,'' Drfurman.com, accessed August 3, 2014, https://www. drfuhrman.com/children/

2 ''EWG's 2014 guide to pesticides in produce,'' Environmental Working Group, accessed August 3, 2014, http://www.ewg.org/foodnews/

3 ''FDA hopes to curb antibiotic use on farms,'' Cable News Network, accessed August 3, 2014, http://www.cnn.com/2013/12/11/health/fda-antibiotics-farms/

4 Dr. Mark Hyman, The UltraMind Solution, page 152

5 Lhkorn99. (2008, August 17). David Wolfe on Superfoods [video file]. Retrieved from, http://rawfoodsplus.com/2010/09/03/david-wolfe-and-the-superfoods/

6 "Leafy Greens Essential for Immune Regulation and Tumor Resolution," Joseph Mercola, accessed August 3, 2014, http://articles.mercola.com/sites/articles/archive/2013/04/08/ eating-sprouts.aspx

7 "Soup-stenance," The Weston A. Price Foundation, accessed August 3, 2014, http://www. westonaprice.org/health-topics/soup-stenance/

8 "Living with Phytic Acid," The Weston A. Price Foundation, accessed on August 3, 2014, http://www.westonaprice.org/health-topics/living-with-phytic-acid/

9 "The Shocking Truth About Freshly Squeezed Orange Juice," Joseph Mercola, accessed August 3, 2014, http://articles.mercola.com/sites/articles/archive/2011/08/16/dirty-little-secret-orange-juice-is-artificially-flavored-to-taste-like-oranges.aspx

Printed in the United States
By Bookmasters